LUCILLE BALL

Essential Lives

LUCILLE

BALL

ACTRESS & COMEDIENNE

by DeAnn Herringshaw

Content Consultant:
Lori Landay, PhD
associate professor of cultural studies, Berklee College of Music

ABDO
Publishing Company

CREDITS

Published by ABDO Publishing Company, 8000 West 78th Street,
Edina, Minnesota 55439. Copyright © 2012 by Abdo Consulting
Group, Inc. International copyrights reserved in all countries.
No part of this book may be reproduced in any form without
written permission from the publisher. The Essential Library™
is a trademark and logo of ABDO Publishing Company.

Printed in the United States of America,
North Mankato, Minnesota
062011
092011

Editor: Mari Kesselring
Copy Editor: Rebecca Rowell
Interior Design and Production: Marie Tupy
Cover Design: Kazuko Collins

Library of Congress Cataloging-in-Publication Data
Herringshaw, DeAnn, 1962-
  Lucille Ball : actress & comedienne / by DeAnn Herringshaw.
     p. cm. -- (Essential lives)
  Includes bibliographical references and index.
  ISBN 978-1-61783-002-0
  1. Ball, Lucille, 1911-1989--Juvenile literature. 2. Entertainers-
-United States--Biography--Juvenile literature. I. Title.
  PN2287.B16H46 2011
  791.4502'8092--dc22
  [B]
                                        2011009392

TABLE OF CONTENTS

Lucille Ball in a 1956 episode of I Love Lucy *titled "Lucy's Italian Movie"*

AMERICA LOVES LUCY

*I*t was Monday evening, January 19, 1953, and more than 44 million people across the United States were watching *I Love Lucy*—the episode in which Lucy Ricardo goes to the hospital and gives birth to a baby boy, Little Ricky. *I Love Lucy* fans had been looking forward to this episode for several weeks. Excitement had been growing since the episode aired in which Lucy tells her husband, Ricky, she is going to have a baby. Lucy and Ricky Ricardo were played by real-life couple Lucille Ball and Desi Arnaz. What made it even more exciting was that Ball, the star of the show, was pregnant in real life.

Ball was already the nation's favorite female comic and *I Love Lucy* was the top show on television, but when her fans found out she was going to have a baby, she became even more beloved. It seemed as though everyone was fascinated with Ball. Newspapers and magazines featured photographs and stories of her, radio shows discussed her pregnancy, and people nationwide were betting on whether her baby would be a boy or a girl. Ball was possibly the most popular expectant mother in the world.

Early Television

The first public demonstration of television excited people at the 1939 World's Fair in New York City. But television did not become part of most Americans' everyday lives until after World War II. By 1948, there were only 6,000 television sets in the United States. As the economy grew during the post-war years, so did Americans' budgets and appetites for fun and entertainment. By the time *I Love Lucy* premiered in October 1951, there were more than 12 million television sets in US homes.

The more than 44 million *I Love Lucy* fans likely had no idea they were making television history that special January night. By tuning in to watch Lucy go to the hospital, they set a new US record for the biggest audience ever to view one television episode. It was well over the size of the audience that tuned in the very next day to watch the inauguration of Dwight D. Eisenhower.

No Pregnancy Allowed

Only a few months earlier, the *I Love Lucy* show had nearly been canceled. When Ball and Arnaz found out Ball was pregnant, they were afraid it would mean the end of their show. It may seem strange to people today, but in the 1950s it was considered improper to show a pregnant woman on television. It had been several years since a pregnant woman had appeared on television. But the producer of *I Love Lucy*, Jess Oppenheimer, had no intention of canceling the most popular television program in the United States. Americans loved Lucy so much he decided to take a chance and write Ball's real-life pregnancy into the show.

Ball and Arnaz were delighted with their producer's decision. Having a baby on the show would open up many possibilities for funny new situations for the Ricardo characters. But they would have to be careful not to offend anyone.

The word *pregnant* was considered taboo, or inappropriate, for a television audience that included children, so the show's writers would have to use the word *expectant* or *expecting* to refer to Lucy's pregnancy. To avoid offending viewers, the show's producers went so far as to ask three clergymen—a Catholic priest, a Protestant minister, and a Jewish rabbi—to check each script and alert the

The Television Code

When television started becoming popular after World War II, there were not many rules about what could be shown. By the 1950s, many people were concerned that some television shows might be harmful to children, especially those featuring crime, horror, sex, and law enforcement. They wanted the government to establish regulations for what could be shown on television, so innocent children would not become corrupted or frightened by offensive programming.

To avoid government censorship of television content, the National Association of Radio and Television Broadcasters created a code in 1952. Networks and local stations would have to enforce the code for all television programs. Breaking the rules of the code could mean that a station could lose its license.

Everyone involved in television production knew breaking the code could mean losing their jobs, so they made more rules that would keep them safe from offending anyone. Because of these rules in the 1950s and 1960s, married couples on television could not be seen sharing a bed. This is why Lucy and Ricky slept in twin beds.

writers to anything that might be objectionable. The clergymen were glad to help, but they never found anything wrong with the scripts.

EXCELLENT TIMING

The night before the record-breaking episode aired, Arnaz took Ball to the hospital to have their second child. Ball had given birth to a little girl, Lucie Desiree Arnaz, a year and a half earlier, just weeks before they started filming the show. While Arnaz was hoping the new baby would be a boy, Ball cared only that the child be healthy. She was so nervous that night she did not sleep at all, but lay awake praying for her baby.

The next morning, Ball went into the delivery room while Arnaz remained in the waiting room. At that time, hospitals did not allow a father in the room where the mother was giving birth. When the baby was born and Ball saw she had

Lucy and *TV Guide*

The first issue of *TV Guide* magazine premiered on April 3, 1953, featuring photographs of Ball and baby Desi on the cover with the headline "Lucy's $50,000,000 Baby." This erroneous and sensational figure was meant to refer to the money Ball and Arnaz's production company, Desilu, was expected to earn from endorsements from their new son. The weekly magazine listed all television programs for the entire week in one slim volume that effectively covered the only three network channels that existed. Ball holds the record for the most appearances on the cover of *TV Guide*: 39.

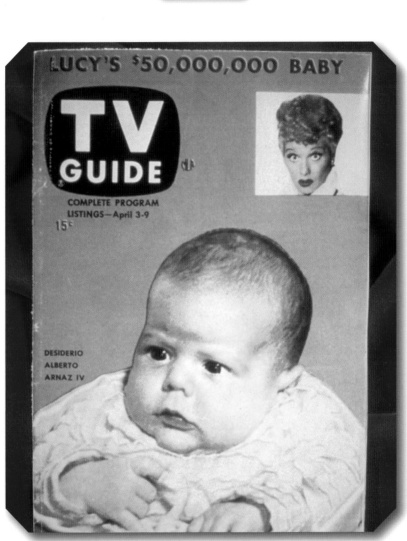

Desi Arnaz Junior appeared on the cover of TV Guide on April 3, 1953. It was the magazine's first issue.

a healthy boy, she was thrilled but exhausted. She said, "His nose is turned up so much he'll drown if it rains—oh, Desi will be so happy!"[1] Then, she fell asleep. When Arnaz heard he had a son, he was more than happy—he was overjoyed. "Now we have everything!" he shouted.[2]

Famous Baby

News of the baby's birth quickly became public and spread all over the world. Crowds of journalists and photographers flocked outside the hospital, but the hospital staff would not let them in. When Ball woke up from her long nap later that day, she found her husband sitting on her bed choked up with emotion. "There were seven thousand letters and a thousand telegrams waiting for me," she later recalled.[3] Gifts of flowers from loving fans filled her hospital room and the halls. Now that fans knew their favorite comedienne and her real-life baby were doing fine, they could sit back and enjoy watching her on their favorite program that night.

Desi Arnaz Jr.

Growing up as the most famous baby in the United States was hard. By 1970, Desi Jr. was a teen idol and the subject of tabloid gossip. He reportedly had affairs with many famous older women. In the 1980s, Desi Jr. worked through a program to achieve sobriety from his dependence on drugs and alcohol. He then became a spokesman for Vernon Howard, whose New Life Foundation self-awareness classes have helped many people. He married dance instructor Amy Bargiel in 1987 and he adopted her daughter, Haley.

Achieving It All

Ball was famous for her excellent comic timing. But the fact that she gave birth to her real-life baby boy and her character gave birth to a baby boy on the very same day was a feat of timing that was truly amazing. While *I Love Lucy* fans watched Ricky's frantic antics as he tried to get Lucy to the hospital on time, Ball and her new baby, Desi Arnaz Junior, were resting safely in the hospital. It was one of the most wonderful and triumphant days of her life, and she had worked hard for it.

Ball had achieved fame, fortune, and family—everything she had always wanted—but she could not banish the fear that somehow she did not deserve such success or happiness. During her most joyful moments, she worried that something terrible would happen and take away her joy and achievements. Although Ball had the ability to make millions of

A Series of Firsts

I Love Lucy was a groundbreaking show in many ways. In an era when television shows were broadcast live, it was the first show to be filmed in front of a studio audience, edited, and broadcast weeks later. This filming technique preserved each episode so that they could be viewed later—thereby inventing the first reruns. It was also the first show to portray a married couple from different ethnic groups. Lucy was Caucasian and Ricky was a Latino from Cuba. And it was the first television show in several years to deal with the sensitive issue of pregnancy and childbirth.

people happy, she had yet to learn to do the same for herself. ⌒

Ball became known not only for her comedic timing but also for her red hair.

Lucille Ball, shortly after her birth in 1911

LITTLE LUCILLE

enry Durrell Ball was a 24-year-old electrician working for a telephone company in Montana in 1910. Desiree Hunt was a pretty and talented pianist who lived in Jamestown, New York. When Henry went to visit his mother and sisters, who also lived in Jamestown, he met the vivacious 18-year-old Desiree. The two quickly fell in love and were married on September 1, 1910. After the wedding, Henry took his bride to live with him in Montana, where Desiree soon became pregnant.

Since Desiree's mother, Flora Belle Hunt, was an expert midwife, Desiree returned to Jamestown so her mother could help deliver her baby. On Sunday, August 6, 1911, Desiree gave birth to a girl she named Lucille Desiree Ball. When Desiree felt strong enough to travel, she took her baby and rejoined her husband in Montana. When Lucille was nearly three years old, the little family moved to a suburb of Detroit, Michigan, where Henry got a job as a foreman for a telephone lineman crew.

Bouncy Baby

Lucille soon became a rambunctious toddler who loved to play rowdy games with her father. Henry would throw Lucille up in the air and catch her and flip her around. Lucille always squealed and laughed with excitement, never showing any sign of fear during these stunts.

When Lucille was three years old, her beloved father became ill with typhoid fever. Desiree was then pregnant with their second child. While she was tending to Henry, Desiree could not watch lively little Lucille.

Early Telephones

In the 1800s, many people were suspicious of telephones. It was hard for them to understand how people could communicate over long distances. Some folks even thought telephones worked by witchcraft or supernatural forces. *The Providence Press* said, "It is hard to resist the notion that the powers of darkness are somehow in league with it."[1] One editorial in the *Boston Times* mocked the invention, saying that "the most serious aspect of this invention is the awful and irresponsible power it will give to the average mother-in-law, who will be able to send her voice around the habitable globe."[2] Other people were excited about the invention of the telephone. They welcomed the new form of communication.

By the time Henry Ball was installing telephone lines in Montana in the early 1900s, many people understood the usefulness of telephones and wanted them installed in their homes and businesses. At that time, all calls had to be placed through an operator. The technology did not exist to allow people to call each other directly, so operators often listened in to other people's conversations.

Installing telephone lines was difficult and dangerous work, but Henry was dedicated. He even went out during a sleet storm when he was sick and climbed icy poles to rehang fallen lines.

To keep her adventurous daughter close by, Desiree tied a dog leash around Lucille's waist and clipped the other end to a pulley on the wire clothesline. As long as Desiree heard the metal runner zipping back and forth on the clothesline, she knew Lucille was safe. But when the backyard grew quiet, Desiree would have to go check on Lucille. Once, she found her smart little girl trying to talk the milkman into untying her: "Mister, help me. I got caught up in this silly clothesline. Can you help me out?"[3]

EARLY SORROW

Unfortunately, Henry's typhoid fever worsened. The doctor came to the house but could do nothing to save him. Henry Ball died on a cold gray day in February 1915. He was only 28 years old. At her father's funeral, Lucille was very quiet and did not show much emotion. But when her father's coffin was lowered into the ground, she began screaming and did not stop until Desiree took her away from the graveyard.

RETURN TO JAMESTOWN

A widow at age 22 and pregnant with a second child, Desiree took Lucille and moved back to Jamestown to live with her parents. Lucille's grandparents, Frederick and Flora

Typhoid Fever

Humans catch typhoid when they consume food or water contaminated with the feces or urine of an infected person. Bacteria that cause typhoid fever, *Salmonella typhi*, attack the intestines, causing fever, abdominal pain, sweating, and rashes. Today, antibiotics exist to treat typhoid and vaccines prevent it. But years ago, many people such as Henry Ball died of this terrible disease because effective treatments were not available. Some people who survive an attack of typhoid may carry the bacteria in their bodies. They can spread the disease if they do not maintain good hygiene and practice careful hand-washing techniques.

Images of Birds

Lucille's first memory was of the day her father died. She remembered her mother weeping, a framed picture falling off the wall, and gazing out a window at some sparrows feeding on a windowsill. Somehow, the little girl associated this moment of deep sorrow and loss with images of birds. For the rest of her life, Lucille could not stand to be in any room that had paintings, photographs, wallpaper, or statues with even one bird on it. Live birds did not bother her—she loved all animals—but she was superstitious about images of birds.

Belle Hunt, were warm and loving people. Their son, Harold, had died of tuberculosis a few years earlier, so when Desiree gave birth to a son in the summer of 1915, Fred and Flora Belle were thrilled to have a boy in the house again. Lucille's new baby brother was named Fred Henry Ball, after his grandfather and father.

Lucille was very jealous of all the attention her brother received. Until his birth, Lucille had been the center of attention, and now she had to share it with baby Fred. But Fred grew into such a kind, respectful, and cheery little boy, Lucille could not help but love him. Lucille and Fred became very close as they grew up.

After Fred's birth, Desiree became increasingly depressed. Her parents decided to send her to California, hoping the change of scenery would cheer her up. Little Freddy stayed with Fred and Flora Belle and Lucille went to live with Desiree's sister

Lola and her husband, George, an immigrant from Greece. Lola and George were very good to Lucille. She later recalled, "Once again I was an only child, with a mother *and* a father, and it was such a happy, relaxed time for me."[4]

Going to California helped revive Desiree's spirit, but she missed her children. After about one year, she returned to Jamestown. Lucille came home to live with her mother.

MOMMY'S NEW HUSBAND

When Lucille was seven years old, Desiree married a man named Ed Peterson on September 17, 1918. Lucille had hoped Ed would be her new father, but he had no such ideas. He would not let Lucille and Freddy call him Daddy.

Soon, he and Desiree moved to Detroit to look for work, leaving Lucille and Freddy behind in Jamestown. Once again, Freddy

Faces in the Mirror

Ed's mother, Grandma Peterson, wanted Lucille to grow up to be a humble, plain, and godly woman. To keep Lucille from becoming vain, Grandma Peterson criticized Lucille's appearance—her long, skinny legs and feet and crooked teeth. She also banished all mirrors from the house, except one in the bathroom. When she caught Lucille studying her facial expressions in that mirror, she punished and shamed the girl. But Lucille was fascinated with making faces, so she sought her reflection elsewhere, such as in trolley car windows, where she practiced making the kind of exaggerated expressions that would make her famous someday.

stayed with Desiree's parents. Instead
of staying with her aunt Lola,
Lucille was sent to stay with her new
stepfather's parents, the Petersons.
Lucille lived with the Petersons for
nearly four years: from ages eight
to 11.

LIVING WITH THE PETERSONS

Unlike the warm and loving
Hunt family, the Petersons were very
religious and strict. They did not
smile or laugh, and they disapproved
of Lucille's high-spirited ways.
Grandma Peterson called anything
fun or exciting "devil's bait" and
believed pleasure was the path to sin
and everlasting damnation.[5] She
assigned many difficult chores that
Lucille hated, and she punished the
girl for the smallest transgression.
Her usual punishment was being
sent to her room, which seemed
like solitary confinement to Lucille.
Often, Lucille did not know what she

Love of Flowers

The only tenderness Lucille ever saw Grandma Peterson show was toward her flower garden. She lovingly tended beautiful daffodils, roses, and dahlias, and passed this appreciation and knowledge to Lucille, who grew up to create her own flower gardens. In later years, Lucille gave Grandma Peterson credit for teaching her self-discipline and how to work hard. She also said, "On the other hand, I have my grandmother Peterson to thank for the gnawing sense of unworthiness and insecurity that haunted me for years. . . . The hardest thing for me was getting used to the idea that I deserved [joy and success]."[6]

When Lucille was 12, her family moved to Celoron. Lucille spent a lot of time visiting Lake Chautauqua.

had done wrong. She experienced many long, lonely hours shut in her room while neighbor children laughed and played outside.

HOME AGAIN

In 1922, when Lucille was nearly 12, Desiree and Ed, who had been living and working in Detroit, returned to Jamestown. Flora Belle was ill with cancer, so Desiree, who now went by the nickname DeDe, came home to help care for her mother and reclaim her children. Grandfather Hunt had recently bought a large house in the country village of Celoron, New York, so now the whole family could live together. The day she left the Peterson house for good, Lucille was excited and relieved. She was going home to her family again. ⌐

Young Lucille Ball, circa 1915. Lucille moved numerous times as a child.

As she grew up, Lucille found she had a dramatic flair and admired vaudeville actors. Buster Keaton was a vaudeville actor whose silent films were popular in the 1920s.

AT HOME IN CELORON

DeDe brought Lucille home to the little white two-story house in Celoron that Grandfather Hunt had purchased for the family. Now, there were eight people living in the house— Grandmother and Grandfather Hunt (the grandkids called him Daddy), DeDe, Ed, Lucille, Freddy, and Lucille's aunt and cousin, Lola and Cleo. But Lucille enjoyed being around family. Although the Hunt family did not have much money, they were rich in love and warmth. Lucille was so happy to be home, she never complained about doing chores or having to watch over Freddy and Cleo. She loved everything about that house, from her little bedroom overlooking the lilacs in the backyard to the landing in front of the staircase. With heavy curtains on one side, that landing became a perfect little stage for Lucille and she put on shows for anyone who would watch.

Lucille's happiness was not complete, however. Soon after she returned home, Lucille learned that her dear grandmother Flora Belle was dying of cancer. This once strong, patient woman wasted away and died in a bed set up for

Vaudeville

For nearly 50 years, vaudeville was the United States' most popular form of entertainment. Vaudeville was a variety show of singing, dancing, comedy, skits, juggling, acrobatics, animal tricks, ventriloquists, magicians, and musicians. These shows went on for hours, with the weakest acts appearing at the beginning and the end.

Many radio, movie, and television stars started in vaudeville. Buster Keaton, Charlie Chaplin, Fred Astaire, the Marx Brothers, Harry Houdini, Jackie Mabley, Bessie Smith, and the Three Stooges all became famous first in vaudeville. Lucille loved watching vaudeville shows and incorporated much of the vaudeville style of comedy into her own routines.

her in the front parlor. Lucille, Freddy, and Cleo were not allowed to attend the funeral, so they held hands and followed the funeral procession down the street, crying inconsolably.

NEW RESPONSIBILITIES

Now that Flora Belle was gone, and since the adults had to work all day, it was up to 12-year-old Lucille to care for the house and two younger children after school. Although she did her best, Lucille was more dramatic than domestic. She spent as much time as she could playacting, only rushing

---

Flora Belle Hunt

Flora Belle Orcutt and her twin were born to a mother who birthed five sets of twins. When their parents died, it looked as though Flora Belle and her siblings would be sent to an orphanage. To help keep the family together, she and her older siblings had to work instead of go to school. She helped raise her younger brothers and sisters and kept everyone organized.

While working as a chambermaid in a hotel, Flora Belle attracted the attention of the owner's son, Fred Hunt. Flora Belle was a beautiful girl and Fred fell in love with her. They soon married and had three children, Harold, Desiree (Lucille's mother), and Lola. Flora Belle became a practical nurse and midwife and was often called to people's homes to help deliver babies and care for the sick.

Despite her hard life, Flora Belle remained open, positive, and loving. She was tenderhearted and had:

a very open, welcoming attitude toward the world. Always cooking, cleaning, sewing, she was a sunny, active, vigorous woman, a dreamer and a planner. Nothing was too much for her, no hours too long, no time better spent than doing things for her family.[1]

through her chores when she knew her mother was coming home. Fortunately, DeDe was not a strict mother and understood Lucille's temperament and good intentions.

Lucille also helped out by getting a summer job at a nearby amusement park where she made and sold hamburgers. She developed a routine in which she would yell out to passersby, "Look out! Look out! Don't step *there!*"[2] When she got their attention, she would say, "Step over *here* and get yourself a de-licious hamburger!"[3] Her technique was often successful, and she worked at the amusement park for several summers.

Tumultuous Teens

Lucille soon grew into a restless, rowdy teenager. She took dares and pulled stunts to get attention, including roller-skating on the gym floor soon after it had been varnished, riding through town on the hood of a boy's car, and not going to school. Lucille also developed a temper. She got into several "kicking, rolling, biting fights on the schoolgrounds" with both boys and girls.[4] Once at school, she even threw a typewriter at her favorite teacher.

Perhaps Lucille was only acting out the tensions growing at home. DeDe and Ed often argued. Grandfather Hunt was unhappy at his job, frequently ranting about how US workers were overworked and underpaid. And DeDe suffered debilitating migraine headaches, which worried Lucille very much.

DRAMA QUEEN

In high school, Lucille began channeling her restless energy into acting. With the encouragement of a teacher, Miss Lillian Appleby, Lucille organized her high school's first dramatic club. She wrote, directed, and starred in a comedy she titled *Charley's Aunt*. The club charged 25¢ a ticket and earned $25, which it donated to the freshman class for a party. After the success of *Charley's Aunt*, Lucille put on several more plays at school and even took part in theatre productions in Jamestown.

Always looking for new ways to express herself and stand out, Lucille was the first girl in her school to cut her hair into the popular boy bob hairstyle—so her girlfriends nicknamed her Bobby. In the 1920s, many parents were scandalized by Lucille's style and behavior. They thought she was wild and out of control.

When Lucille was 14 years old, she fell in love for the first time—with a 21-year-old named Johnny DeVita. Johnny drove her around town in his car and took her to see vaudeville shows. Lucille loved the DeVita family, who adored her as well. Johnny was rumored to have connections with gangsters, but Lucille did not care. DeDe, who was usually a very permissive mother, told Johnny to stay away from Lucille. But it did not work. The two spent time together anyway.

The Gunshot

The summer when Lucille was nearly 16 years old, Grandfather Hunt gave a .22-caliber rifle to Freddy for his twelfth birthday. Grandfather Hunt set up a tin-can target on the edge of the yard with open fields beyond so the bullets would not go near any houses or streets. Then, he carefully instructed

Desiree or DeDe

Fred and Flora Belle Hunt named their first daughter Desire. When she got older, Desire changed her name to Desiree. When Cleo was learning to talk, she began calling Desiree "DeDe," and the nickname stuck. DeDe liked her new name so much she went by it for the rest of her life.

DeDe felt guilty for the time she was away from her children, so she tried to make up for those lost years. She became president of the school's parent-teacher association and made costumes for Lucille's plays.

Fred Hunt

Fred Hunt had many jobs. His first job was working in his father's hotel. He also worked for the post office delivering mail, ran a grocery store, and made optical instruments for eye doctors. Fred was a skilled woodworker but could not make enough money as a fine crafts-man, so he had to work in a furniture factory operat-ing a lathe. At one point, Hunt studied to become a chiropractor. Although he was not able to make a living as a chiropractor, his neighbors called him Doctor because he used his skills to help anyone who had an aching back.

Freddy in gun safety rules. After Freddy fired a few times, his friend, a girl named Johanna who was visiting from out of town, wanted a turn. Grandfather Hunt showed her how to shoot and then stood nearby observing. Soon, Cleo's friend, a neighbor boy named Warner Erickson, came to watch. Grandfather Hunt told him to sit down and stay out of the way, but when Warner heard his mother calling him, he jumped up and ran for home—crossing the path between the gun and the target right as Johanna pulled the trigger. Warner fell bleeding to the ground. He was rushed to the hospital.

The next day, they learned the terrible news that Warner's spinal cord had been severed by the small bullet. He would be paralyzed from the waist down for the rest of his life. He would never walk again. Johanna, the girl who fired the gun, went into shock after the accident. She returned to her home out of state and never saw Lucille or her family again.

LEAVING CELORON

Warner's mother sued Grandfather Hunt for negligence, saying he should have prevented the disaster. She won her suit and Grandfather Hunt had to pay her his life savings and declare bankruptcy. Soon Mrs. Erickson sued him again for more money, and won again. As a result, Grandfather Hunt had to sell the family's beloved home. He was also sentenced to a year in jail, which devastated him.

Losing the family home and everything he had worked for was hard for Lucille's grandfather. Even more difficult was the loss of his good name in the community. And no amount of money could make Warner walk again, which was very sad for Lucille's family. They all liked Warner very much.

Aunt Lola's Shop

Lola and George divorced when Cleo was a baby, so Lola and Cleo moved in with Fred and Flora Belle. Needing to earn money while staying home with Cleo, Lola operated a beauty shop in one part of the house. Lucille loved helping in the beauty shop. Sometimes, Lola's customers brought their children along. While Lola was busy with the mothers, Lucille often cut and styled their children's hair. Unfortunately, Lucille's attempts were often disastrous and Lola went out of business. Lola did not seem to mind much and instead went to school to become a nurse like her mother.

Lucille, who had seen the accident happen, became suspicious of the US justice system after the incident. She did not believe the punishment her grandfather received was fair. She was horrified when the law came and took the house and everything in it. Dispirited and broken, Lucille and her family moved to a small apartment in Jamestown to try to start over.

Lucille cut her hair into a bob, a women's hairstyle
that was popular in the 1920s.

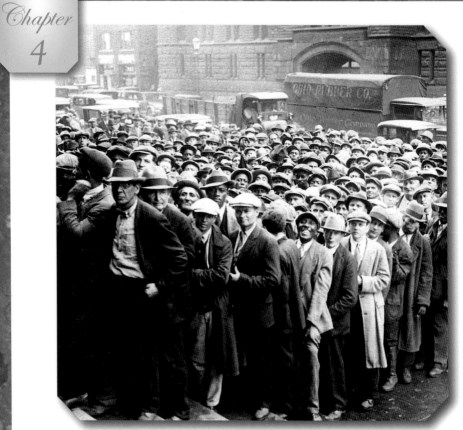

People gather in Cleveland hoping to find jobs.
The stock market crash of 1929 triggered the Great Depression,
a time of widespread unemployment.

LEAVING HOME

After moving to Jamestown, Lucille became even more restless. She hated her new high school in Jamestown, where she began her junior year. Soon, she began running away to bigger cities—Chicago, Buffalo, and Cleveland.

When she was home, Lucille would borrow Johnny DeVita's car and drive recklessly at high speeds. DeDe worried about her wayward daughter and wanted some way of guiding her while allowing her freedom and self-expression. One evening at dinner, DeDe told Lucille she had borrowed money from the bank to send her daughter to drama school in New York City. Lucille was ecstatic.

Lucille was 17 when she began studying at the John Murray Anderson-Robert Milton School of Drama. On her first day, both her teacher and her fellow students laughed at her country pronunciations and mannerisms. The more her instructors criticized her, the more introverted she became. She already knew she could not sing or dance well, but now she could not even be funny anymore. Everyone ignored her. At the end of the term, Lucille was sent away. The school sent DeDe a letter saying her daughter had no talent or future as an actress.

DRAMATIC DROPOUT

Determined to make it in show business, Lucille did not return to Jamestown. There were parts for hundreds of pretty girls to parade on Broadway

Diane Belmont

When Lucille first began modeling, she used the name Diane Belmont. She had always thought the name Diane was elegant, and she chose Belmont for the horse racing track on New York's Long Island. After Lucille became a famous actress, many of her old friends who knew Lucille in her modeling days thought Hollywood changed her name to Lucille Ball. They did not realize Diane Belmont was not Lucille's real name.

stages in elaborate outfits of feathers, fur, and sequins, so she decided to become a showgirl. Lucille was very poor during this time. She lived in a ratty little rooming house, and often went hungry. Sometimes, she even took leftover doughnuts that restaurant customers left behind or begged strangers for bus money. Finally, Lucille got a small background part in a big show. She did four more showgirl parts but was fired from a sixth show because she could not dance ballet.

Despite her setbacks, Lucille knew she would make it in show business someday. In the meantime, she got a job modeling coats and clothing. Not only was she able to earn enough money to support herself, she began to learn poise and confidence and honed a keen fashion sense. But Lucille suffered from homesickness and missed her mother terribly. Over the next two or three years, she

New York City in the early 1930s

would go back and forth between New York City and
Jamestown several times. She was still seeing Johnny
DeVita during this time as well.

DIFFICULT TIMES

Lucille's aunt Lola was working as a nurse in the summer of 1930 when she died unexpectedly from an acute case of peritonitis caused by a dangerous infection in the abdomen. The family was devastated. Lola was only 32 years old. After the funeral, Lola's ex-husband, George, came to take Cleo away to live with him and his family. This was doubly devastating, especially for DeDe and Lucille, who adored Cleo. Lucille cried inconsolably, afraid she would never see her cousin again.

After Lola's death, DeDe and Ed separated and divorced. Lucille returned to her modeling job in New York City. Brother Fred moved in as well, sharing her apartment while he finished high school in the big city. Not long afterward, DeDe and Grandfather Hunt moved to New York, and they all got an apartment together. This was during the early years of the Great Depression, when many people had no jobs. Grandfather Hunt was horrified by the poverty in New York City. Automobiles sat for weeks in the streets because people had no money for gasoline. Grandfather Hunt, an ardent Socialist, had never trusted the unbridled capitalism that ran the US economy. Now in his early sixties, he could not find work. He became as despondent as the men he saw in the streets.

Lucille was proud to be able to help her family during these difficult times. She knew she was lucky to have steady modeling work that paid her a living wage and allowed her to meet so many interesting people. Although times were hard, Lucille always found ways to have fun, even at work while modeling. High-spirited and pretty, she still liked to clown around and make people laugh. This not only helped sell clothes, it attracted many men who enjoyed her

High Fashion Modeling

After starting as a wholesale coat model, Lucille worked her way into high fashion modeling. Her first such job was working in Hattie Carnegie's famous brownstone salon on East Forty-Ninth Street. "Hattie taught me how to slouch properly in a $1,000 hand-sewn sequin dress and how to wear a $40,000 sable coat as casually as rabbit,"[1] Lucille said. Carnegie also freely pinched her young model in the ribs to make her stand up straight. She even kicked Lucille in the shins so she would remember not to lock her knees. Lucille did not mind this because Carnegie was also very warm and caring. She even sent Lucille to her own doctor when Lucille was stricken with a sudden strange illness.

Lucille's best—and last—modeling job was at a clothing design house called Jacksons. The designer there was Rosie Roth, Carnegie's former partner. Jacksons paid Roth $25,000 a year, a very high salary for a female designer in the 1930s. When Lucille grew bored at work, she would clown around while Roth complained, "You got flair, you got personality, a beautiful body you got . . . so why you so aggravating? You make my ulcer ache."[2]

company and would take her out to expensive restaurants and exclusive parties.

The Mysterious Illness

While modeling in New York, Lucille contracted a mysterious illness that left her legs very weak. When she returned to Jamestown to recover, she wore heavy orthotic shoes to help rebuild leg muscle. Years later, she claimed it had been rheumatoid arthritis that paralyzed her for three months. Her cure, she said, came through nutrition, rest, and experimental injections of "horse serum."[3]

Lucille's friends and family assert she was not paralyzed; she was ill from malnutrition and overwork. She may have had rheumatic fever, which could have weakened her legs, but she could not have had rheumatoid arthritis, a lifelong affliction.

CHESTERFIELD GIRL'S BIG BREAK

By the time Lucille was 20, she was fairly well-known in the fashion industry. She made friends with photographers and artists, acting agents and directors. One of her artist friends painted a portrait of her in a sophisticated yellow gown with a pair of Russian wolfhounds. He sold the painting to the Chesterfield cigarette company, which put Lucille's portrait on billboards all over the United States. Lucille's face became famous overnight. When a Goldwyn Studios movie producer recognized Lucille as the latest Chesterfield girl, he hired her to be in the movie *Roman Scandals*, starring Eddie Cantor. Lucille could hardly believe it—she was going to Hollywood.

Lucille appears in an advertisement for the film Roman Scandals *in 1933.*

Ball drinks a cup of coffee with producer William Cagney in Hollywood in 1933.

QUEEN OF THE BS

Ball was one of only 12 pretty young women hired to play slave girls in *Roman Scandals* in 1933. Unlike the others, who wanted to be seen as glamorous, Ball focused on being noticed. She volunteered for any stunt, such as getting mud splattered in her face for the camera. She soon became known for being a good sport who would do anything for laughs. To her, this job at Goldwyn Studios was a learning experience. She expected to return to New York in a few weeks.

A California Home

But instead of going home, Ball signed a six-month contract with Goldwyn, playing bit parts and chorus girls. She then became a contract player for Columbia Pictures and later for RKO. By this time, Ball had decided that Hollywood was the place to be. She was earning a steady salary—and she was also scrimping and saving every penny, determined to bring her whole family to live with her in California.

While other starlets bought themselves fancy clothes and cars, Ball rode a bike to work, dreaming of the day when she could have

Grandpa the Socialist

Grandfather Hunt carried his socialism to new heights in California. In the 1930s, the Socialist Party had between 10,000 and 20,000 members. Hunt hosted Communist meetings in the family home, bragging that his granddaughter, the actress Lucille Ball, was happy to open her home to the Communist Party. Ball was too busy working to pay attention to her grandfather's activities. She loved him dearly and humored him when she could, so when he asked her to join the Socialist Party or sign petitions, she did—merely to pacify him, not because she believed in his causes. Ball had never been interested in politics and seldom got around to voting.

Lela's Little Theatre

Lela Rogers ran a workshop called the Little Theatre. She put on plays, rehearsing with her pupils strictly. She made them read literature and taught them how to dress and behave for auditions.

One director told Lela not to waste time on Ball, saying she would never amount to anything. But Lela saw Ball's potential "as a clown with glamour" and helped the budding actress refine her look and voice.[1] Lela told Ball she could make her a star in two years if Ball worked hard enough and faithfully followed Lela's advice. Later, Ball credited her success to Lela's firm guidance.

her loved ones nearby. Soon, her brother joined her. Together, she and Fred fixed up and decorated a three-bedroom house. Within a few months, DeDe, Grandfather Hunt, and Cleo also moved in. Ball finally had her family together again.

PERFECTING HER CRAFT

By 1935, Ball was still playing small movie parts and wondering when she would make it big in show business. Then, she met Lela Rogers. Lela had worked hard to make her own daughter a star—and she succeeded. Her daughter was the famous Ginger Rogers who costarred in many Hollywood hits with the renowned dancer Fred Astaire. Ball was playing another background showgirl part in one of these films when she struck up a friendship with Ginger Rogers. Ginger and her mother, Lela, were very close, so when Ginger made a new friend, Lela did, too. Lela also had the

Fred Astaire and Ginger Rogers appeared in many films together in the 1930s.

habit of taking aspiring actors under her wing, helping them learn how to survive in the cutthroat world of Hollywood. With Lela's coaching and encouragement,

Ball honed her acting craft and began getting larger roles.

She also began getting work in radio. In 1938, Ball played comic female parts in several radio programs where she had to use tone of voice and timing to convey meaning and humor. Doing radio helped Ball perfect these skills—she developed a reputation as an up-and-coming comedienne.

B Movies

So-called B movies were low-budget films featuring lesser-known actors. A-list movies starred big-name stars and were promoted aggressively. During the Great Depression, moviegoers expected to get more than one movie for the price of a ticket, so going to the movies meant seeing a newsreel and cartoons first, a B movie next, and then an A movie as the main feature.

Always Hungry

Unlike many movie performers who had to diet to keep trim, Ball had to eat hearty meals to keep on weight. Her personal maid, Harriet McCain, accompanied Ball to movie sets and cooked big breakfasts of "steak, fried potatoes, hot biscuits—the works."[2] Later in the day, Ball would send her maid to fetch a fried-potato sandwich from the commissary wagon.

Ball often got irritable when she was hungry. After one of Ball's temperamental outbursts on set, McCain would apologize to the cast and crew for her boss's behavior, saying, "Miss Ball didn't mean it. . . . She's just hungry."[3]

During the late 1930s and early 1940s, Ball made so many B movies she became known as the "Queen of the Bs."[4] In these films, she often played wisecracking career girls, tough mistresses, or flustered wives. Although few of these films were big hits, producers and directors took notice of Ball's unique talents, especially her comedic timing.

The 1939 film *Five Came Back*, in which Ball played a supporting role, actually became a critical and box office hit. After the success of *Five Came Back*, producers and directors began seeing Ball as A-movie material. Ball began to believe she would make it big very soon.

ENTER DESI ARNAZ

The fun-loving Ball had dated many men in New York and Hollywood, but she had never been seriously in love with anyone since Johnny DeVita. Although she wanted to have a family of her own someday, she had not yet found a man she wanted to marry. Then in 1940, while in Hollywood making the movie *Dance, Girl, Dance*, Ball met a young Cuban musician and actor named Desi Arnaz. The two fell wildly in love almost immediately.

Arnaz had grown up in a rich and powerful family in Cuba. After the Batista revolution, Arnaz fled his homeland on a boat in 1935 and landed, impoverished, in Miami, Florida. He worked cleaning birdcages, driving a banana truck, and playing drums in a Latin band. Handsome, engaging, and quick to learn, Arnaz managed to support himself and his parents with his Latin nightclub acts. Latin music was the latest craze in the 1930s and Arnaz was an enthusiastic performer. He drew large crowds to the clubs and

Batista Revolution

Desiderio Arnaz y de Acha II was a doctor and the mayor of Santiago, Cuba. He married a rich and beautiful heiress named Dolores. Desiderio and Dolores had one son, Desiderio Alberto Arnaz y de Acha III, nicknamed Desi, who grew up knowing only comfort and wealth. When Desi was 16 years old, he had his own speedboat, a car, and many horses. Popular with women, Desi could do almost anything he wanted—then came the 1933 Batista revolution.

Cuba had seen many uprisings over the years due to the vast divide between rich and poor—the powerful and the powerless. Desi was 16 years old when Fulgencio Batista led a revolt, overthrowing Cuba's power structure. As a member of the ruling elite, Desi's father was imprisoned with the Cuban Senate, their properties confiscated. When revolutionaries came to the Arnaz ranch, looting and burning everything, Desi and his mother fled for their lives disguised as peasants. The Arnaz family lost everything they owned and had to hide in Havana with relatives. Finally, Desi's father was released from prison. He escaped to Miami, where Desi and Delores soon joined him. At one point, they were so poor they had to live in a rat-infested warehouse.

helped make the conga line a wildly popular dance.

He was then offered a role in a 1939 Broadway play *Too Many Girls* as a bongo-playing college student. The play was a big hit. When *Too Many Girls* was adapted for the screen the next year, Arnaz went along with the director to Hollywood. There, Arnaz met Ball, who was in costume and makeup after performing a fight scene in another movie called *Dance, Girl, Dance*. She had a black eye and wore a tacky, torn costume. Arnaz was not impressed at all. He thought she looked terrible.

Later that day, he met her again and did not recognize her. She was cleaned up and wearing a cute outfit. Arnaz thought she was very attractive and was amazed to find out she was the same person he had met earlier that day. They went out for dinner and dancing with friends and spent hours together talking.

Almost Instant Love

Ball and Arnaz claimed they did not fall in love at first sight—but the people who were there that day disagreed. Movie star Maureen O'Hara witnessed Ball meeting Arnaz. "It was like Wow! A bolt of lightning! Lucille fell like a ton of bricks."[5] And a friend of Arnaz said, "They hit it off right away."[6]

Later that evening, listening to Arnaz tell his life story, Ball realized what was happening. "I fell in love with Desi wham, bang! In five minutes. There was only one thing better than looking at Desi, and that was talking to him."[7]

Only a few days after they met, Arnaz broke off his engagement to a dancer named Renee DeMarco, and Ball broke up with Alexander Hall, the movie director she had been dating steadily for five years. Ball had finally met the man she wanted to marry. ⌐

Lucille Ball

In the 1930s, Ball developed her career
through working on radio programs.

By 1940, Ball was experiencing success in her career as an actress.

Early Marriage

all and Arnaz's romance was passionate and often interrupted by work. When they were apart, Arnaz sent Ball many telegrams professing his undying love for her and often called saying how much he missed her. Despite their mutual love and attraction for each other, they frequently quarreled, usually over her allegations of his unfaithfulness, some of which were true.

Too Many Differences

Ball and Arnaz also had very different backgrounds and ways of viewing the world. One evening, they sat in a restaurant and listed all the reasons why they should never marry. After that meeting, the two decided to go separate ways, and Ball thought it was over between them. She had promised her friends and colleagues she would not marry Arnaz, saying they both knew it was impossible and inadvisable. She even gave an interview for a magazine article titled "Why I Will Always Remain a Bachelor Girl."[1]

Persistence Pays Off

But Arnaz refused to give up Ball. He continued sending telegrams and calling her while they were traveling on separate projects. Finally, after a few weeks of this, Ball agreed to elope with Arnaz.

On the morning of November 30, 1940, Ball and Arnaz were married by a justice of the peace in Greenwich, Connecticut. Arnaz had a show to perform that night, so they had to drive quickly back to New York. On the road that day, they heard on the radio the news of their elopement. When they arrived at the theatre where Arnaz was to perform, reporters and photographers mobbed them. The media was already fascinated with the newlyweds.

Home on the Ranch

A few months after their marriage, Ball and Arnaz bought a house on five acres (2 ha) in the San Fernando Valley of California. They wanted a retreat from the crazy life of Hollywood— somewhere they

---

Reasons Not to Marry

Ball and Arnaz listed many reasons they should never marry each other. Ball was six years older, which bothered her greatly. She grew up poor and white. Arnaz grew up rich and Latino. She was Protestant. He was Catholic. She lived moderately, saving money, drinking little—he gambled, spent to excess, and drank. Their work kept them apart, preventing them from building a life together. She was independent and career focused. He wanted a wife who would stay at home. Ball admired Arnaz but doubted her ability to make him happy.

Ball and Arnaz quarreled dramatically. DeDe often mediated their spats. Eventually, the two would calm down and ardently make up. But when DeDe was not around, their tempers often took over.

On one occasion, Ball smashed all the windows in their brand new car. Arnaz once threw a tantrum in front of party guests when Ball accidentally made him feel foolish. Another time, Ball found a cigarette lighter that looked like a pistol. She pointed the thing at Arnaz's chest and pulled the trigger. A flame appeared, so Arnaz casually lit a cigarette and walked out on her.

Arnaz carried Ball over a dressing-room threshold on the day they eloped in 1940.

could raise a family. Ball gloried in decorating the house and Arnaz built a swimming pool, pool house, and Cuban-style barbecue kitchen outdoors.

They had chickens, a cow, pigs, and dogs—and to make their ranch complete, they fused their names and christened their property *Desilu*.

The romantic couple loved to entertain friends and relatives at their ranch and often held big parties. Both continued to work and gain respect in the business, but complete happiness eluded them. They wanted children, but Ball seemed to have trouble getting pregnant. When she finally did get pregnant, she miscarried.

THE NEW LOOK

In 1942, after finally starring in A-list films and winning admiration from critics, Ball's contract with RKO was over. She got a new contract now with Metro-Goldwyn-Mayer (MGM), a more prestigious studio. But Ball was overwhelmed by the change. The people at RKO had been a second family to her and she knew everyone's names. At MGM,

Telegrams from Arnaz

During their frequent separations, Arnaz often sent telegrams to Ball. "Darling, things look swell. I miss you so much and I'm awfully sorry if I was mean the other night but I love you so much I guess I lost my head. Darling, it was wonderful talking to you tonight but awful when I hung up and was left alone . . . Love, Desi"[2]

In another telegram, he said, "Sweetheart, it is wonderful to know exactly what one wants. These few weeks away from you have been very sad and painful, but they have showed me that I want you and you always."[3]

she underwent a nerve-wracking makeover that lasted for hours. The hair designer decided to color her mousy brown locks a vibrant red, but, unfortunately, it turned out green. The stylists had to work for hours to get her hair the right color of red.

The next day, makeup artists chose new colors for her lips, eyelids, and cheeks. They gave her long feathery false eyelashes and enhanced her scanty eyebrows. This was when Ball's trademark "'Lucy Look' was born."[4]

MORE PERFORMANCES

With this new look, Ball starred in the lavish MGM musical production of *Du Barry was a Lady*, which was a huge hit. She then made a comedy titled *Best Foot Forward*. Critics and audiences alike raved about the films and Ball's performances.

Meanwhile Arnaz's professional life was not doing as well. Worried

"I believe that we are as happy in life as we make up our minds to be. All actors and actresses, no matter how talented or famous, have ups and downs in their careers. It's just the nature of the business. You have to learn to roll with the punches, and not take them personally."[5]
—*Lucille Ball*

about her husband's career, Ball voiced her concern. Finally, the head of MGM, Louis B. Mayer, offered Arnaz a good part in the film *Bataan.* Arnaz accepted the offer. Although Arnaz won the *Photoplay* magazine award for best performance of the month, MGM would not give him any more roles.

THE ALMOST DIVORCE

The year 1944 was a difficult one for Ball. In January, her grandfather Hunt died of a stroke, so she and DeDe flew to Jamestown to bury him beside his wife, Flora Belle. Ball's dreams of having a baby had not materialized and Arnaz rarely came home to the Desilu ranch. She knew he was being unfaithful to her, despite his many promises of love. Eventually, weary of these separations, their fights, and the lack of marital stability, Ball filed for divorce.

Staff Sergeant Arnaz

After Arnaz became a US citizen in 1943, he was drafted into the air force for World War II (1939–1945). A knee injury kept him from combat duty, so he was in charge of entertaining the troops—a job in which he excelled. His connections in the entertainment business allowed Arnaz access to many stars, including Ball, who often made appearances at the base. It also made for good publicity for the players. During that era of strong national pride, Americans admired stars who contributed to the war effort by boosting the morale of the troops.

But the night before the divorce was to go into effect, Arnaz and Ball reconciled. They each took responsibility for contributing to their marriage problems. Jealousy, flares of temper, and self-centeredness had no place in a good marriage. Ball decided to accept the fact that Arnaz would likely continue dallying with other women. Instead of blaming Arnaz for the affairs, she took to blaming other women for tempting him.

A New Project

In 1944, Arnaz moved back home to Desilu ranch. The two decided they needed to find an acting project they could do together. If they saw each other all day and came home together every night, perhaps Arnaz would not have so many opportunities to cheat. Costarring in a movie became their dearest wish— but they were not sure how to make

Macho Man

Arnaz grew up in a home where the husband ruled the household. Arnaz carried these expectations into his marriage to Ball. He became furious on their wedding night when he found out Ball had been out and about while he was performing. "I won't have my wife riding around New York *alone* in a taxi!"[6]

Later that night, he woke Ball from a sound sleep and told her he wanted her to fetch him a glass of water. Ball later explained, "I was out of bed and running the tap in the bathroom before I woke sufficiently to wonder why in the [world] he didn't get it himself."[7]

that happen. In the end, their quest for projects they could do together would lead them to their best acting opportunity yet.

Although on the verge of divorce in 1944,
Ball and Arnaz decided to work on their marriage.

Ball and Arnaz dressed up to attend a hospital benefit in 1948.

THE LEGEND OF LUCY

*B*all continued to work steadily in film and stage throughout the 1940s. But her aspirations of having children and costarring with her husband in a movie continued to elude her. Arnaz's movie career had stalled since he had been away in the military for two and a half years, and the studios did not want him back. So, he revived his Latin nightclub act and went on the road. Ball and Arnaz were once again separated due to work.

In 1948, Ball starred in a radio situation comedy show called *My Favorite Husband*, in which she played a scatterbrained wife who gets into all kinds of scrapes. The show became very popular and was a huge success.

In 1949, Ball and Arnaz decided to work harder on making their marriage successful. Ball promised to be more understanding and Arnaz promised to take only local nightclub engagements—no more cross-country tours. Staying together and having children became their top priority. They even held a ceremony in a local Catholic church to renew their vows.

DESILU PRODUCTIONS

In 1950, Ball and Arnaz took a big risk and created their own production company so they could realize their dream of costarring together. They called their company Desilu Productions Inc. and began working on a husband-and-wife comedy routine with the brilliant writers from *My Favorite*

Husband: Jess Oppenheimer, Madelyn Pugh, and Bob Carroll Jr.

Arnaz played a Latin bandleader who sang and played bongos; Ball played his wife who kept trying to get in on the act with her silly stunts. The couple took the vaudeville-style act on the road and audiences loved them.

The couple was even happier when they found out Ball was pregnant. Unfortunately, she miscarried after three months. Although she was heartbroken, Ball soon became pregnant again. At nearly 40 years of age, Ball decided to take better care of herself to make sure she did not lose this

The President of Desilu

Many people thought Arnaz was merely a Cuban drummer who was lucky to have a talented wife. But Ball knew better. She made sure the *I Love Lucy* team knew it, too. Since her career had been more successful than his, Ball was happy to let Arnaz take the lead at Desilu.

Arnaz firmly set down the principles of the show: the humor would not be sarcastic or cruel, Ricky and Lucy would be faithful to each other, mother-in-law jokes were forbidden, and Ricky would never be seen as ridiculous. "When Lucy's got something up her sleeve that would make Ricky look like a fool, let the audience know that I'm in on the secret," Arnaz told the writers.[1]

According to Ball,

Desi was a great showman, but many were surprised to learn he was a genius with keen instincts for comedy and plot. He has a quick, brilliant mind; he can instantly find the flaw in any story line; and he has inherent good taste and an intuitive knowledge of what will and will not play. He is a great producer, a great director.[2]

baby. Arnaz also became more devoted and careful not to upset his wife.

CREATING LUCY

When she was four months pregnant, Ball and Arnaz finally received the offer they had dreamed of: CBS would give them a spot to do a television situation comedy based on their vaudeville routine. At first, the studio did not want Arnaz to play the part of Ball's husband. They did not think the US public wanted to see a white woman with a Latino husband. But the popular Ball-Arnaz vaudeville act convinced the company's conservative businessmen otherwise.

Ball and Arnaz called in their favorite writers—Oppenheimer, Pugh, and Carroll—to help come up with a script. As they all worked together on developing Ball's on-screen character, Arnaz said, "'She tries so hard . . . she can't dance and she can't sing . . . she's earnest and pathetic . . . Oh, I love that Lucy!'"[3] And that was how the famous show got its name.

"The best year of my marriage to Desi was just before and after the birth of our first child. We exchanged no harsh words and experienced no upsets of any kind. Desi hovered about me, attentive to every need. I was grateful . . . and in a complete daze of happiness. . . . Desi had a yellow convertible he usually drove at seventy and eighty miles an hour. As soon as he learned I was expecting again, he began driving [like] an old lady."[4]

—*Lucille Ball*

As the writers developed the Lucy and Ricky Ricardo characters, they also began looking for actors to play Fred and Ethel Mertz, Lucy and Ricky's neighbors. The actor they wanted to play Fred had other commitments, so William Frawley was chosen for the part. Ball was not very happy about this choice and even more dubious about Vivian Vance, who would play Ethel. Vance was 39, a year younger than Ball. Ball thought she did not look dumpy enough to be Fred's wife. Vance assured Ball she could play a frumpy character, and Ball reluctantly agreed. She was also impressed with Vance's professionalism and perfectionism. However, Vance and Frawley did not like each other from the start. While this made for tension behind the scenes, it also made Fred and Ethel's on-screen scrapping believable.

Lights! Camera!

The main obstacle for Desilu Productions was figuring out how to film the show in front of a live

Vivian Vance

Born Vivian Roberta Jones in 1909 in Kansas, Vivian Vance studied theatre and music in Kansas and in Albuquerque, New Mexico. She was a gifted singer and actress. When Arnaz saw her perform on stage, he immediately offered her the role of Ethel Mertz.

Vance suffered a nervous breakdown in the 1940s. She attributed her recovery to psychotherapy and learning to develop a tranquil state of mind. She often played peacemaker when tempers flared on the *I Love Lucy* set and had a calming influence on everyone around her.

After three divorces, Vance finally married happily. She died of bone cancer in 1979.

audience. Until this point, live television shows were caught on kinescope and sent all over the United States. Kinescope produced a fuzzy picture, which Arnaz did not want. So, Arnaz worked with some of the best cameramen in the business and adopted a solution using three cameras, one for close-ups, one for medium shots, and one for distance, following the action. This would give film editors more shots to choose from when cutting and splicing the film into a show. Arnaz rented an unused movie studio where he built four different sets: one for each room in the Ricardo's apartment and a fourth that could be adapted into Ricky's nightclub or other locations as needed. In order to accommodate an audience of 300 people, Arnaz built bleachers, restrooms, and water fountains.

Ball and Arnaz personally approved every item of decoration for the Ricardo's home—down to the last pillow and plate. During this time, Ball was the

William Frawley

William Frawley was born in 1887 in Burlington, Iowa. He performed vaudeville musical comedy for many years. He and his wife, Edna Louise Broedt, toured with their *Frawley and Louise* act until they divorced in 1927.

In 1932, Frawley moved to Hollywood and worked for Paramount. By the time he got the role of Fred Mertz, Frawley had appeared in more than 100 films. When *I Love Lucy* ended, he worked for five years on *My Three Sons,* but his failing health forced him to retire. He died of a heart attack on March 3, 1966, at the age of 79.

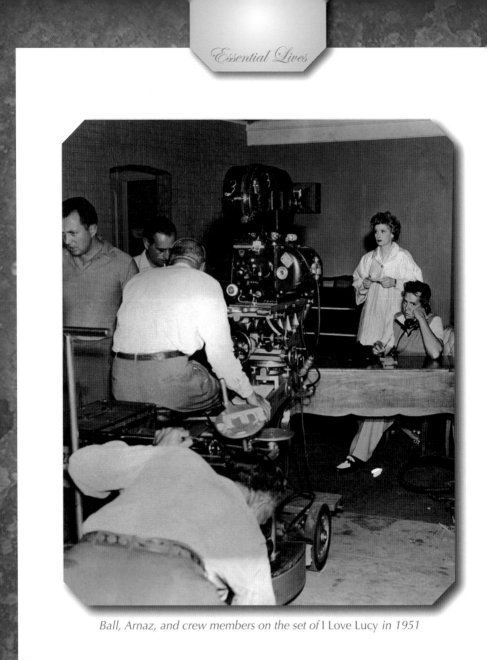

Ball, Arnaz, and crew members on the set of I Love Lucy *in 1951*

happiest she had ever been. She was realizing her two greatest dreams—and the most important to her was having a baby. Arnaz built an addition onto their ranch home to accommodate the new baby and a nurse, while Ball oversaw decorating. She believed motherhood would bring out the best in her.

Action!

On July 17, 1951, Ball's first child was delivered by caesarean section. She had wanted to give birth naturally, but the baby's position made that impossible. When Ball awoke from the anesthesia, the nurse told the new mother she had a baby girl. Ball had decided to name the baby Susan if it were a girl, so she asked the nurse to bring her Susan. "You mean Lucie," the nurse said as she laid the baby in Ball's arms.[5] While Ball was sleeping, her husband had written the name Lucie on the birth certificate as a surprise. Ball was ecstatic and lay in bed gazing adoringly at her daughter.

Six weeks after Lucie's birth, Ball returned to work to begin rehearsals.

Personal Perfection

Ball was delighted to discover that doing *I Love Lucy* allowed her to use all the skills she had developed over the years. Everything she learned in vaudeville, modeling, radio, movies, and theater was put to use. And the perfectionism she learned from Grandma Peterson came in handy as well. Ball explained, "I wanted everything about the venture to be top-flight: the timing, the handling of props, the dialogue. We argued a good deal at first because we all cared so passionately; sometimes we'd discuss phrasing or word emphasis in a line of dialogue until past midnight."[6]

The 1950s Household

Part of the reason audiences loved *I Love Lucy* was because the comedy reflected their own day-to-day lives. In the 1950s, most women were housewives, like Lucy. They stayed at home, taking care of the house and the children, while their husbands worked. Husbands were generally expected to make the rules for their household, including how money would be spent. For example, in *I Love Lucy,* Ricky provides Lucy with an allowance to purchase groceries and other things for the house. Viewers enjoyed watching a comedy that showcased things that were important to them.

In the fall of 1951, Desilu filmed its first episode of *I Love Lucy* in front of a live audience. Arnaz had explained to the audience in the bleachers they would be seeing a new kind of show and how the filming worked. He introduced the cast and greeted family and friends in the audience. The actors took their places and the show began. This first episode was called "Lucy Thinks Ricky is Trying to Murder Her," an idea Lucy gets from reading crime novels. The audience responded, laughing heartily as Lucy created a makeshift bulletproof vest with a cast iron skillet.

I Love Lucy was an almost instant hit. After only four shows, it made the list of top ten television shows. By its twentieth episode, *I Love Lucy* was the number one show in the United States—and it stayed at number one from 1952 to 1954. Ball and Arnaz had succeeded beyond their wildest dreams.

Desi Arnaz in 1955. On I Love Lucy, *Arnaz was able to showcase his musical talent.*

Ball, Arnaz, and Lucie with Arnaz's mother, left,
and Ball's mother, right, in 1952

DEALING WITH SUCCESS

Many actors dream of success, but too much success at once can be overwhelming. That is what Ball found out after finishing the first wildly triumphant season of *I Love Lucy*. She and Arnaz had achieved so much so quickly—parenthood, a production company, and the number one television show in the country. In 1952, it became almost too much to bear.

Seeking Help

Ball briefly sought psychiatric help to better cope with the mounting pressures. She wanted to learn to control her temperamental outbursts and her deep-seated fears she had to protect her territory or everything good would be taken from her. Ball's doctor helped her learn to distance herself from problems and not react so strongly when things did not go her way.

Ball also met and consulted with Dr. Norman Vincent Peale, a popular minister and author of the book *The Power of Positive Thinking*. He listened to Ball relate her fears that she would lose her success just as her family had lost everything in Celoron. Peale encouraged Ball to remain positive, noting that even if she did fail, she could always rebuild it all again because "her success was

The Wrong Red

In 1952, Ball received her first Emmy nomination for excellence in comedy. She and Arnaz attended the award show, but the statue went to Red Skelton, who had worked with Ball years earlier. When he received the award, Skelton said, "Ladies and Gentlemen, you've given this to the wrong redhead. I don't deserve this. It should go to Lucille Ball."[1] Skelton reduced Ball and the audience to tears when he tried to give the statue to her. Skelton remained good friends with Ball for many years.

in herself."[2] Ball cried with relief to hear this. She consulted Peale for many years.

The Red Scare

In 1953, the famous redhead was falsely accused of being another kind of red—a Communist. In 1936, Ball had registered as a member of the Communist Party to please Grandfather Hunt, though she disagreed with his politics. Both the FBI and the House Un-American Activities Committee questioned the star for hours, but they cleared her of suspicion because she had never voted. Unfortunately, Ball's secret hearing was leaked to the media. Soon, the country was buzzing with suspicions about the famous comedienne.

Ball was beside herself with worry. After the gunshot accident in Celoron, she knew how people's suspicions could lead to another's

McCarthyism

During the 1940s and 1950s, Americans feared that Communists would take over the world. Senator Joseph McCarthy stirred up these fears and accused many people of being Communists. It was similar to a witch hunt—and writers, artists, and entertainers were a favorite target. Anyone suspected of Communist activities could be interrogated by the Un-American Activities Committee and pressured to name other Communists. If they resisted, the accused could be jailed or blacklisted, which meant they would never work again. These attitudes and activities were called McCarthyism. For fear of being accused themselves, few members of the press spoke out against McCarthy or McCarthyism.

ruin. Fortunately, US government officials announced to the press that Ball was innocent. Certain members of the media apologized to Ball, her fans were very supportive, and *I Love Lucy* remained as popular as ever for several seasons. Ball was very lucky that she was already such a popular star. Many actors' careers were completely ruined when they were accused of being Communists.

DESILU EXPANDS

In February 1953, shortly after Desi Jr.'s birth, Ball and Arnaz accepted an Emmy for *I Love Lucy* as the best situation

Getting Sponsored

In the 1950s, television could not happen without sponsors. Sponsors are companies that sell products or services—anything from soap to cars to soda pop. These companies pay a great deal of money to have television shows play their advertisements during a program. The more popular the program, the more expensive it is to buy a commercial spot.

The money sponsors pay to a show provides for nearly everything that goes into it—salaries for cast and crew, costumes, sets, and film—so, in many ways, a television show is at the mercy of its sponsors. If a company ends its sponsorship, the show could be canceled. Sponsors may pull their ads if the show does not have enough viewers or if too many people get angry about something in the show and threaten to boycott the company's products unless it stops sponsoring that show.

When Ball was accused of being a Communist, everyone at Desilu was afraid sponsor Phillip Morris would call off its sponsorship. If that happened, the show would be canceled, which could have meant the end of Ball's career. But after a top representative at Phillip Morris spoke to Arnaz and read Ball's testimony, the company decided to stand by her.

Ball appears in a scene from The Long, Long Trailer.
The movie gave Ball a chance to display her skill in physical comedy.

comedy. At this time, Desilu began producing
other television shows as well. Together, the famous
couple made a motion picture called *The Long, Long*

Trailer. Desilu also opened a merchandising business. Stores began selling all kinds of *I Love Lucy* goods: furniture, home accessories, clothing, kitchenware, dolls, games, and jewelry. The company was making so much money from selling merchandise, people called it "Desiloot."[3] Arnaz and Ball became very busy with the company's expansion. To shorten their commute between home and work, Ball and Arnaz sold the Desilu ranch in the country and bought a big house in Beverley Hills in 1954. In 1957, Desilu purchased RKO—the studio company where Ball had been "Queen of the Bs." Now, their production company was one of the biggest in the business.

Pressures Build

Ball and Arnaz loved their work, but huge success brought huge pressures. A power struggle erupted between Arnaz and Oppenheimer over executive producer responsibilities and credit. Though Ball may have tried to remain calm and positive, she often flew into tantrums at home and on the set. Arnaz, who had always been a heavy drinker, became dependent on alcohol to cope. He had always been respectful and even-tempered at work, but now he showed up stumbling drunk, bursting into rages over petty issues. His gambling, excessive spending, and carousing with women continued, which caused friction in the couple's marriage—and in their work. Ball and Arnaz became more and more estranged. Ironically, doing a show together did not ultimately bring them closer—it drove them apart.

> "Viv and I . . . both believe wholeheartedly in what we call 'an enchanted sense of play,' and use it liberally. . . . It's a happy frame of mind, the light touch, skipping into things instead of plodding. It's looking at things from a child's point of view and believing. The only way I can play a funny scene is to believe it. Then I can convincingly eat like a dog under a table, freeze to death beneath burning-hot klieg lights, or bake a loaf of bread ten feet long."[4]
>
> —Lucille Ball

The End of Lucy

The half-hour *I Love Lucy* show ran for six seasons, from 1951 to 1957. It lasted 179 episodes. Then, Ball and Arnaz decided to cut back their hectic work schedules. They created the *Lucy-Desi Comedy Hour*, a monthly special instead of a weekly program, which ran from 1957 to 1960.

The year 1960 was not only the end of the *I Love Lucy* characters; it was also the end of Ball and Arnaz's marriage. They were divorced on May 3, 1960. Arnaz's heavy drinking was destroying his health, his relationships, and his desire to work. He soon retired to his horse ranch.

From left, James Cagney, Bob Hope, Ball, and Arnaz in 1956. Ball and Arnaz divorced in 1960.

NEW BEGINNINGS

But Ball kept working as hard as ever. In 1960, she made a movie with Bob Hope called *The Facts of Life*. Then, she went to New York to realize her dream of starring on Broadway. She headlined in the musical comedy *Wildcat*. Despite her hard work and an excellent cast, *Wildcat* received poor reviews.

Ball drove herself too hard and became very ill. After she collapsed on stage, she was hospitalized for exhaustion and the show closed.

When Ball recovered her health, she also gained hope. She had been devastated by her failed marriage to Arnaz, but now she had a new love interest. While in New York, she had met a tall, handsome stand-up comedian named Gary Morton. He had never seen a single episode of *I Love Lucy*. Confident yet cool, Morton was not intimidated by Ball's fame, fortune, or brusque mannerisms. When she was with Morton, Ball felt relaxed—more like her true and best self.

Morton soon joined Ball in California and befriended Lucie and Desi Jr. After he proposed marriage several times, Ball finally accepted. On November 19, 1961, Ball and Morton were married. Dr. Norman Vincent Peale, Ball's spiritual mentor, performed the ceremony.

"The entire project rode on the radiant talent of that woman. [She] was a simply . . . stunning performer. In every sense, she was a star. . . . Ask her for royalty and she became a queen. And she kept astounding us that way each week. . . . There was no feeling that the audience was watching her act. She simply was Lucy Ricardo. . . . Every fiber in [her] body was contributing to the illusion. Did Ricky catch her in a lie? She wouldn't be just a voice denying it. Her stance would be a liar's stance . . . hands . . . feet . . . knees . . . would be doing just the right thing."[5]

—Jess Oppenheimer, head writer of I Love Lucy

Ball and Morton, 1961

Vance and Ball in an episode of The Lucy Show, *which ran from 1962 to 1968*

THE LATER YEARS

Following her wedding to Morton, Ball was finally beginning to relax at home and enjoy her new husband. After so many years of frustration, Ball finally felt capable of happiness again. But this newfound tranquility would be short-lived.

The Lucy Show

In spring of 1962, Arnaz called with an idea for a new Desilu production. It would be a television show based on the novel *Life Without George* by Irene Kampen, about two single mothers raising their children together, called *The Lucy Show*. Ball immediately contacted Vance and begged her to costar. Vance was reluctant. She had recently remarried as well and was very happy with her new husband in Connecticut. But Ball offered such a good salary, Vance could not refuse.

Gale Gordon, an old friend of Ball, also costarred in the show that began filming that fall. And Ball gave Lucie and Desi Jr. bit parts in the show so she could spend more time with them.

Ball Buys Desilu

Although Ball and Arnaz were learning to coexist peacefully in their new separate lives, Ball found it impossible to have both her new and old husband working together on

Like before Love

After her marriage to Morton, Ball realized she and Arnaz had never really liked each other. They had passion and chemistry, and they were very much in love, but their values and interests differed greatly. They both disapproved of each other in many ways. Because they could not accept each other, they tried to change each other—an impossible task. Ball learned not to do this in her next relationship. Regarding her courtship with Morton, she said, "We liked each other before we loved each other. We approve of each other; neither of us is trying to change the other."[1]

The Lucy Show. In November 1962, Ball bought Arnaz's share of Desilu for $3 million. She became the first woman to own and head her own major studio and production company.

With Ball as president, Desilu became known for taking chances on more innovative, exciting programming. The most famous of these shows were the original *Star Trek* and *Mission Impossible* in 1966 and *Mannix* in 1967.

A Lesser Lucy

The Lucy Show, which ran from 1962 to 1968, tried to rekindle the magic Ball and Vance had on *I Love Lucy.* Although audiences still loved Lucy, many critics did not. They thought Ball had embodied Lucy Ricardo beautifully; the funny situations she got into sprang from her genuineness as a character. But Lucy Carmichael, the new character, was "stupidly incompetent."[2] Her predicaments were simply silly for the sake of being silly. It was as though Ball was not creating a real character with Lucy Carmichael. She mugged for the camera, but her gags did not make sense to the storyline.

But Ball did not enjoy being an executive. She was a performer at heart, and the pressures of running Desilu were too much for her. In 1967, she sold Desilu Productions to Charles D. Bluhdorn, who had purchased Paramount Pictures a year earlier. She then formed Lucille Ball Productions, which would produce only her projects. Morton was vice president of this much smaller company.

More Lucy

In 1968, *The Lucy Show* ended. Ball then starred with Henry Fonda in the

Ball in a scene from 1968's Yours, Mine, and Ours

hit motion picture *Yours, Mine, and Ours*. In this film,
Ball played a widow with eight children who marries
a widower with ten children, and together they have

another baby. Later that year, Ball started another new series, *Here's Lucy*, featuring herself and her two teenagers played by her real-life children, Lucie and Desi Jr. *Here's Lucy* ran from 1968 to 1974.

Ball had become increasingly concerned about her children, especially Desi Jr., who at a young age had started his own rock band and began experimenting with alcohol and drugs. Although working with their mother gave the Arnaz children excellent experience in show business, they were not turning out the way their mother had hoped.

Lucie moved into her own apartment as soon as she turned 18 in 1969. She wanted a life away from the chaos and drama her mother seemed to create everywhere. At 19 years old, Lucie married her high school sweetheart against her mother's wishes. The marriage lasted one year. Ball never seemed to get over her daughter's youthful mistakes and publicly mocked Lucie's early failures even decades later.

Lucie Arnaz

Although Lucie and her famous mother had their differences, they did grow closer over the years. In 1979, Lucie starred in the Broadway musical *They're Playing Our Song*. Ball was immensely proud of her talented daughter. In 1980, Lucie married Laurence Luckinbill, an actor 17 years older than she. Lucie and Luckinbill gave Ball and Arnaz three grandchildren.

Lucie learned from her mother's mistakes to put children before career. She has given lectures about balancing parent-hood and performing. "When you choose to have a busy career and a family, a lot of confusing things happen in your life. When you're home, you have to be really home."[3]

The Ski Accident

Ball loved to snow ski. In 1972, she was standing at the bottom of a slope when a woman on skis crashed into her. Ball's right leg was broken in four places. The physical pain was excruciating, but the emotional pain was worse and she despaired over the loss of her physical strength and beauty. This happened right when she wanted very much to take on a new film project called *Mame*, a musical about a wealthy woman who becomes guardian of her brother's child. After she was back on her feet, and against the advice of friend and colleagues, Ball starred in *Mame*, which came out in 1974. It was an abysmal failure. The film was shot in very soft focus, and Ball came off looking ridiculous.

No More Lucy

After *Here's Lucy* ended, Ball made a few special appearances, but she spent most of her time at home. When her mother, DeDe, died in July 1977, Ball was desolate. DeDe once said she hoped her daughter died first because she did not know how Ball would survive without her.

Ball did not like to be seen in public because she did not like to see people's reactions to the way she

Ball and singer Ray Charles attended an awards event at the White House in 1986.

was aging. One day when she was out shopping, a little girl who recognized Ball as Lucy asked her what happened to her face. Ball was crushed.

Then in 1985, she was offered an opportunity to play the part of a homeless woman in a made-for-television movie called *Stone Pillow*. It was a dramatic role, not a funny one, and Ball thought she would be doing something important by making it. Unfortunately, most critics and audiences did not like the movie. In *Stone Pillow*, Ball's character was not comedic. People expected Ball to make them laugh, so she tried to do that one more time.

In 1986, at the urging of her husband and colleagues, she tried to revive a Lucy-like character in a new situation comedy, *Life with Lucy*, in which she played a goofy grandmother. After it premiered, reviews and ratings were terrible. People mocked her for trying to do the same kind of gags she had always done. The show was canceled after eight episodes. Ball was devastated again.

Good-bye, Desi

A few weeks later, on December 2, 1986, Arnaz died of lung cancer. His funeral was small—only Ball and those who had been closest to him attended. Over the years, after their divorce, Ball and Arnaz had become friends. They were able to share the joy of children and grandchildren without fighting. Ball was thankful for that, but she knew her own time was growing short.

Final Triumphs

Ball's life seemed to be made up of strange patterns where extreme sorrows and successes followed each other regularly. Right after Arnaz's death, Ball was invited by President Ronald Reagan to receive the Kennedy Center Award. She went to Washington DC on December 7 to accept the most prestigious award given to US entertainers.

On May 10, 1988, Ball had a stroke and was rushed to the hospital. She was partially paralyzed on her right side and her speech was very slurred. Over the next few months, she worked hard in physical therapy and gradually regained her speech and ability to move.

In March 1989, she was invited to appear on stage with Bob Hope at the Oscars ceremony. As she walked on stage wearing an exquisite gown, arm-in-arm with Hope, the audience of their colleagues gave the duo a long and appreciative standing ovation. It was vindication for Ball to have Hollywood's best and brightest recognize and appreciate her for her body of work, despite her latest flops.

FAREWELL, FUNNY LADY

A month later, Ball awoke one morning in severe pain. She had a torn aorta and damaged heart valve, but she came through the surgery to patch her aorta. During the next week, her fans flooded the hospital with get-well cards and telephone calls wishing her a speedy recovery. Ball was thrilled to know so many people still loved her. She seemed to be healing well, but on April 26, 1989, on the morning she was to go home, the patched aorta burst and she died. Ball was 77 years old.

Newspapers across the United States published long obituaries about the nation's favorite comedienne. People held memorial services and television shows made tributes to her memory. Her body was cremated and Morton, Lucie, and Desi Jr. interred her ashes at Forest Lawn Memorial Park in Hollywood Hills, as she had requested. Then in 2002, Ball's children had her ashes removed and buried in Lake View Cemetery in Jamestown, New York, near Ball's family.

The Lucy-Desi Center

Located in Ball's hometown of Jamestown, New York, the Lucy-Desi Center consists of a museum, a gift shop, and the Desilu Playhouse. The Lucy-Desi Center's mission is to "preserve and celebrate the legacy of Lucille Ball and Desi Arnaz and enrich the world through the healing powers of love and laughter."[4] The center puts on two festivals per year in Jamestown—one for Ball's birthday in August and another called Lucy-Desi Days during Memorial Day weekend. Both festivals offer many attractions for families, including contests, celebrity events, movie showings, and music.

The Desilu Playhouse offers recreations of Lucy and Ricky's apartment and several other famous sets. It also displays props and costumes used by the *I Love Lucy* cast. Hundreds of fans from all over the world visit the Lucy-Desi Center each year.

The Lucy Legacy Lives

Lucille Ball lived an extraordinary life. She was a woman of contrast and contradictions. With a great capacity for love and warmth, she could also be cold and distant. Despite her flaws, she remains a television icon—in 1984, she became the first woman inducted into the Television Hall of Fame. She overcame poverty, insecurity, and early abandonment to succeed as a model, an actress on stage and screen, and finally to become the first lady of comedy. Her comic timing is still recognized as genius. Comedians today study her techniques with great respect. Her legacy of laughter lives on in film and television. It is no wonder so many people still love Lucy. ⌐

Lucille Ball

33
usa

2001

© 2000 USPS   PRELIMINARY DESIGN

Issued in 2001, a US postal stamp honors Ball
in a set called the Legends of Hollywood.

TIMELINE

1911

Lucille Desiree Ball is born in Jamestown, New York, on August 6, 1911.

1915

In February, Ball's father, Henry Ball, dies of typhoid fever.

1928

Ball briefly attends drama school in New York City.

1950

Ball and Arnaz form their own production company, Desilu Productions Inc.

1951

Ball gives birth to a daughter, Lucie, on July 17.

1951

Desilu Productions films the first episode of *I Love Lucy* in the fall.

1933

Ball moves
to Hollywood
and begins a film
acting career.

1940

Ball marries
Desi Arnaz
on November 30.

1948

Ball stars
in the radio program
My Favorite Husband.

1952

Ball receives her first
Emmy nomination
for excellence in
comedy. The award
goes to Red Skelton.

1953

Ball is accused
of being
a Communist.

1953

More than 44 million
viewers tune in to
I Love Lucy
on January 19
for Little Ricky's
birth, the birthday
of Ball's actual son.

TIMELINE

1953

In February,
I Love Lucy wins
an Emmy for best
situation comedy.

1953

TV Guide magazine
premieres on
April 3, 1953,
featuring photographs
of Ball and baby
Desi Jr. on the cover.

1957

New episodes of
I Love Lucy
stop airing.

1962

In November,
Ball buys Desilu
Productions from
Arnaz, making Ball
the first woman to
head a major
production company.

1968

The Lucy Show
ends and Ball begins
a new television
series, *Here's Lucy*.

1984

Ball is the first
woman inducted
into the Television
Hall of Fame.

Lucille Ball

1960	1961	1962
Ball and Arnaz divorce on May 3.	On November 19, Ball marries Gary Morton.	In the fall, *The Lucy Show* begins.

1986	1986	1989
Life with Lucy premieres but is canceled after eight episodes.	On December 7, Ball receives the Kennedy Center Award in Washington DC.	Ball dies on April 26.

Essential Facts

Date of Birth
August 6, 1911

Place of Birth
Jamestown, New York

Date of Death
April 26, 1989

Parents
Henry Durrell and Desiree Hunt Ball

Education
John Murray Anderson-Robert Milton School of Drama

Marriages
Desiderio Alberto Arnaz y de Acha III (1940–1960),
Gary Morton (1961)

Children
Lucie Desiree Arnaz
Desi Arnaz Jr.

Career Highlights

Ball began her acting career in the 1930s doing walk-on and bit parts in movies. She went from playing supporting to starring roles in many low budget films and finally in A-list films. Ball performed in the hit radio program *My Favorite Husband* from 1948 to 1951. In 1951, she and husband Desi Arnaz created Desilu Productions and the *I Love Lucy* show, which became the most popular television show in the United States. Ball was the first woman to own a major production company. She went on to win many awards for her brilliant acting and comedy techniques.

Societal Contribution

Ball's comic timing, gifts of pantomime and slapstick, and wide range of facial expressions continue to inspire performers. Many modern comedians study her techniques to create their own brand of humor.

Conflicts

Throughout her life, Ball struggled with the fear that her success would be taken from her. She was a perfectionist and often lost her temper when others did not meet her expectations. Balancing marriage, parenthood, and work was difficult for her. In 1953, Ball was accused of being a Communist.

Quote

"I believe that we are as happy in life as we make up our minds to be. All actors and actresses, no matter how talented or famous, have ups and downs in their careers. It's just the nature of the business. You have to learn to roll with the punches, and not take them personally."—*Lucille Ball*

Glossary

aorta
> The largest artery in the body; blood moves from the heart through the aorta to all parts of the body.

bit part
> In acting, a supporting role with at least one line of dialogue.

capitalism
> An economic system based on the buying and selling of goods and services; protects private property.

commissary
> A lunchroom on a movie set where cast and crew members can buy food.

Communist
> A person who supports an economic system based on sharing goods and services as needed and in which private property is eliminated.

contract player
> An actor hired by a production studio to perform in a certain number of movies or for a certain number of years.

elite
> People of the highest class or with the most power in a society.

living wage
> The minimum amount of money needed to fulfill a person's basic needs for food, housing, clothing, transportation, health care, and recreation.

negligence
> Failure to take the proper care to prevent injury to someone else.

pacify
> To bring peace or calm.

pantomime
> The art of portraying emotions by using only gestures, without speech.

perfectionism
> A personal standard in which anything less than perfect is unacceptable.

slapstick
> A comedy technique that uses sight gags such as pies in the face, stepping on banana peels, falling down, and so on.

unbridled
> Unrestrained; out of control.

vivacious
> Lively and spirited.

ADDITIONAL RESOURCES

SELECTED BIBLIOGRAPHY

Ball, Lucille. *Love, Lucy*. New York: Putnam, 1996. Print.

Brady, Kathleen. *The Life of Lucille Ball*. New York: Hyperion, 1994. Print.

Sanders, Coyne Steven, and Tom Gilbert. *Desilu: The Story of Lucille Ball and Desi Arnaz*. New York: Morrow, 1993. Print.

FURTHER READINGS

Edwards, Elisabeth. *I Love Lucy: Celebrating 50 Years of Love and Laughter*. Philadelphia: Running, 2010. Print.

Karol, Michael. *Lucy A to Z: The Lucille Ball Encyclopedia*. Lincoln, NE: iUniverse, 2004. Print.

Woog, Adam. *Lucille Ball*. Farmington Mills, MI: Lucent, 2002. Print.

Yapp, Nick. *Lucille Ball*. London: Endeavour, 2010. Print.

Web Links

To learn more about Lucille Ball, visit ABDO Publishing Company online at **www.abdopublishing.com**. Web sites about Lucille Ball are featured on our Book Links page. These links are routinely monitored and updated to provide the most current information available.

Places to Visit

Lucille Ball-Desi Arnaz Center Inc.
2 West Third Street, Jamestown, NY 14701
716-484-0800
http://lucy-desi.com
Through its museum and playhouse, the center strives to preserve the memory of Lucille Ball and Desi Arnaz as well as promote comedy.

Television Hall of Fame
Academy of Television Arts and Sciences
5220 Lankershim Boulevard, North Hollywood, CA 91601
818-754-2800
http://www.emmys.tv/awards/hall-fame
This museum features statues of Lucille Ball and many other famous celebrities.

Source Notes

Chapter 1. America Loves Lucy
1. Coyne Steven Sanders and Tom Gilbert. *Desilu: The Story of Lucille Ball and Desi Arnaz.* New York: Morrow, 1993. Print. 68.
2. Ibid. 69.
3. Lucille Ball. *Love, Lucy.* New York: Putnam, 1996. Print. 222.

Chapter 2. Little Lucille
1. "Chapter II.-The Building of Business." *The Free Library.* Farlex, 2010. Web. 14 Dec. 2010.
2. Ibid.
3. Kathleen Brady. *The Life of Lucille Ball.* New York: Hyperion, 1994. Print. 6.
4. Lucille Ball. *Love, Lucy.* New York: Putnam, 1996. 9.
5. Lucille Ball. *Love, Lucy.* New York: Putnam, 1996. Print. 10.
6. Ibid. 12.

Chapter 3. At Home in Celoron
1. Lucille Ball. *Love, Lucy*. New York: Putnam, 1996. Print. 14.
2. Ibid. 31.
3. Ibid.
4. Ibid. 26.

Chapter 4. Leaving Home
1. Lucille Ball. *Love, Lucy*. New York: Putnam, 1996. Print. 54.
2. Ibid. 67.
3. Ibid. 57.

Chapter 5. Queen of the Bs
1. Lucille Ball. *Love, Lucy*. New York: Putnam, 1996. Print. 90.
2. Ibid. 112.
3. Ibid.. 113.
4. Kathleen Brady. *The Life of Lucille Ball*. New York: Hyperion, 1994. Print. 85.
5. Ibid. 102.
6. Ibid. 103.
7. Lucille Ball. *Love, Lucy*. New York: Putnam, 1996. Print. 117.

Chapter 6. Early Marriage
1. Lucille Ball. *Love, Lucy*. New York: Putnam, 1996. Print. 133.
2. Ibid. 128.
3. Ibid.
4. Kathleen Brady. *The Life of Lucille Ball*. New York: Hyperion, 1994. Print. 133.
5. Lucille Ball. *Love, Lucy*. New York: Putnam, 1996. Print. 107.
6. Ibid. 136.
7. Ibid. 137.

Chapter 7. The Legend of Lucy
1. Lucille Ball. *Love, Lucy*. New York: Putnam, 1996. Print. 207.
2. Ibid.
3. Ibid.
4. Ibid. 203.
5. Stefan Kanfer. *Balls of Fire: The Tumultuous Life and Comic Art of Lucille Ball*. New York: Vintage, 2003. Print. 133.
6. Lucille Ball. *Love, Lucy*. New York: Putnam, 1996. Print. 213.

Chapter 8. Dealing with Success

1. Coyne Steven Sanders and Tom Gilbert. *Desilu: The Story of Lucille Ball and Desi Arnaz*. New York: Morrow, 1993. Print. 58.

2. Kathleen Brady. *The Life of Lucille Ball*. New York: Hyperion, 1994. Print. 209.

3. Coyne Steven Sanders and Tom Gilbert. *Desilu: The Story of Lucille Ball and Desi Arnaz*. New York: Morrow, 1993. Print. 71.

4. Lucille Ball. *Love, Lucy*. New York: Putnam, 1996. Print. 208.

5. Coyne Steven Sanders and Tom Gilbert. *Desilu: The Story of Lucille Ball and Desi Arnaz*. New York: Morrow, 1993. Print. 52–53.

Chapter 9. The Later Years

1. Lucille Ball. *Love, Lucy*. New York: Putnam, 1996. Print. 273.

2. Kathleen Brady. *The Life of Lucille Ball*. New York: Hyperion, 1994. Print. 298.

3. Paul Hodgins. "Finding a Balance Stage: Learning from Her Mother's Career, Lucie Arnaz Decided Acting Would Take a Back Seat to Parenthood." *Orange County Register*. LucieArnaz.com, 2010. Web. 14 Dec. 2010.

4. "Our Purpose, Our Mission." *Lucy-Desi.com*. Lucille Ball-Desi Arnaz Center, Inc., 2008. Web. 14 Dec. 2010.

INDEX

ABOUT THE AUTHOR

DeAnn Herringshaw has been working as a writer, editor, and
writing consultant for educational and non-profit organizations
for more than 15 years. She especially enjoys doing research because
she loves the challenge of learning and sharing new ideas. She lives
in Minnesota.

PHOTO CREDITS